LOST SIGNAL

Palimpsest Press
1171 Eastlawn Ave.
Windsor, Ontario. N8S 3J1
www.palimpsestpress.ca

Printed and bound in Canada
Cover design and book typography by Ellie Hastings
Edited by Jim Johnstone
Cover art by Joseph Siddiqi

Palimpsest Press would like to thank the Canada Council for the Arts and the Ontario Arts Council for their support of our publishing program. We also acknowledge the assistance of the Government of Ontario through the Ontario Book Publishing Tax Credit.

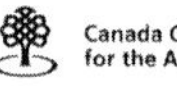

Canadä

LIBRARY AND ARCHIVES CANADA CATALOGUING IN PUBLICATION

TITLE: Lost signal : poems / Chris Hutchinson.
NAMES: Hutchinson, Chris, 1972- author
IDENTIFIERS: Canadiana (print) 20250182696
Canadiana (ebook) 20250182726

ISBN 9781990293917 (SOFTCOVER)
ISBN 9781990293955 (EPUB)
SUBJECTS: LCGFT: Poetry.
CLASSIFICATION: LCC PS8615.U823 L67 2025 | DDC C811/.6—DC23

poems

CHRIS HUTCHINSON

CONTENTS

ONE

TWO

THREE

FOUR

For Teresa McWhirter

ONE

Everybody gets so much information all day long that they lose their common sense.

— Gertrude Stein

Lost Signal

Ping me with your promises
from decades down the tracks.
Sing me off to sleep.
Tonight, I'm a surgeon
cutting myself open
with the virtual edge of this screen.

Remember how I died, as a child, from riches?
Poverty, not poetry, brought me back to life.
Need came first, then strife

then spirit flooding in, reversed limelight
spilling shadow-shapes
across the page.

Tonight, I'm on a train
of thought that follows a famous river
into this feeling of mirrors and unread books

into twilight and old usages.
You're just radio waves.
I'm the touch of a touchscreen

away. Please reply before I fall asleep
again. Promise to write my name
on the crumbling Empire's sky

with your spire-like pen.

What I Want Isn't Always What I Want to Want

I want the sunflower's star power
and reckless ambition.

(((( ))))

I want to believe I want
all sentient beings to be free
from suffering, and the causes of suffering.

(((( ))))

Sifting through my father's ashes
I want his gold molars.

(((( ))))

Digging deeper
I want to crack open
my own ribs, refashion them
as trellises for mycelia, centipedes
and underground streams.

(((( ))))

Yes, I want to walk
the Stoic's path, but only once
I'm robed in purple and crowned
in emeralds and amethysts.

Who doesn't want to know
if they're sleeping when they're awake
if they're dreaming when they're at home
or if they've become insane
in the vicinity of riches?

Who doesn't want to fall
into the future's unblinking eye
into a circle with no circumference
no centre?

Yes, I want to swap bodies
with my long August shadow
but only to stride alongside Modigliani's
thin-necked women.

No more better living
through manufactured vaccines.
Instead, I want a promise
the next manufactured plague
is not a fait accompli.

((((·))))

No more probable knowledge
automated systems
of thought, the human mind entrained
by that which claims to be the end
of want, of shame, of history.

((((·))))

Some confessions are penned
without a single point of punctuation.
Wanting for nothing, some lives
are sadly blessed.

((((·))))

I'd rather be cursed
like a field of sunflowers
seething with seeds
under a night full of stars.

Treason Season

Again, your iridescent beetle
tunneling under my rhododendrons

is hungry for those slick
wriggly nightcrawlers

twisting themselves
into ampersands

Celtic knots
molecular diagrams

of black widow venom
and crypto-anarcho ciphers

of late October's sweet
lemony rot.

In each case, your cupidity
is stupid, but so is pulling the ripcord

on my backup discourse
at this particular moment

in post-pandemic mudslinging
history. Filthy, horrid Floridian

begone! The double exposure of your DKE
photo ID is just another symbol

of symbology, a lowkey metaphor
for metaphoricity, like the image

of a spherical virus magnified
to the size of the magnifying glass

through which I'm gazing
at a dandelion gone to seed.

You with me? Can you sense
the pointless passing of time

each moment swooping in
from a new direction

with a new missive of misinformation
clenched like a dead red rose

in its teeth? Can you see how
my reinvented days of the week

Sundress, Money, Tulip, Weiner dog, Thyroid, Famine, Satirize
are nothing but a joke to themselves

resembling a flurry of bodies cartwheeling
down the burning halls of academe?

But now — before a Starlink satellite train appears
like a tiki torch parade fiery enough

to burn down the whole internet —
let's move back to the shady

rainy, willow of the valley side
of my garden fantasies

where the Kingdom of Fungi
once withstood the seditious hordes

with their billy goat beards
ancient flip phones, and bad cuneiform

tattoos, where you once exhumed
my long-lost doppelganger's

decomposing corpse — didn't you? —
and your jewel-bedizened scarab

went tunneling under my rhododendrons.

Waving from the Shores of Key West

From far away, dear ocean
your crashing breakers sound like the ghosts
of refugees playing kettledrum-sized
tambourines.

Your distant mists
must be dreaming of matrices
made from grayscale pixels
smaller than fish eggs

yet profuse enough to obscure
these bodies like glass bottles
with never-to-be-read messages washing up
along your limestone shore.

But let's think back before
this poem — how the urtext
of the calm, uninjured page resisted
every bullet, every point, every food-for-thought chestnut

then marrying off its offspring
then leasing out its depths
to your interplay of light, silence
and glitchy eellike shadows.

Then what? And who am I to say?
And aren't we all just shipwrecked here
in the same squelchy, pedestrian
dream?

Up close, dear ocean
dear Wallace Stevens on ecstasy, I can see
the ice-cream hills and morphing alphabets
of your sunlit crests forever

sliding off the slippery brows of smiling
dolphins, smiling because they are happy
to be swimming free of hills and alphabets
without the human need of hands or feet.

Who am I, trying to mimic
your motions, contain your currents
of grief? And what does it mean
to drown standing safely

on shore, waving my arms
as if signalling in crazy semaphores
each stanza — *look!* — unfurling here
like a tiny wind-torn flag?

X

My soul has wings —
just like the one-legged, one-eyed

seagull in a strip mall parking lot
pecking at empty, cherry-red

french-fry sleeves, surrounded by
other wingèd souls

with traffic cone beaks
that dumbly jab and snap

at the small knot
of his knee, at the surrendering

flag of his tailfeathers
and honk and shriek until

he finally turns
toward the sea and

flies away.

Hope (Vancouver, 2003 - 2023)

> *"Hope" is the thing with feathers —*
> *That perches in the soul —*
> *And sings the tune without the words —*
> *And never stops — at all —*
> — Emily Dickinson

Back then, my autobiography was purely speculative
except for those final pages about feathery things

of light — how they leapt up from behind the Mayor's
sky-blue, blood-pimpled dumpsters

behind his new urban living community planted
like a luxury cruise ship, bow-first into the ground

then flew off like sightless swans beyond
the Salish Sea.

Back then, when I wasn't looking, those final pages
must've written themselves, because now I've forgotten

the faraway, ocean-decayed metropolis I once lived in
motherland of Marxist apologists, cross-eyed Siamese cats

yowling on Eastvan streets spotted with penny-sized
track marks of rain, and in the distance, prehistoric mountains

like green white-capped waves frozen on the verge
of washing all of our money and wasted pain forever

and never away.

We Dream Again of Psalm 137

After dropping the planet-sized
skulls we are trying

to juggle in our sleep
the ensuing thunder summons the history

of wars and occupations.
Each lost soul, reclaimed, its lust

for vengeance masquerading
as devotion to god and state — rages

suffered, suffused, transfigured
into art. It's always thus. The captors

request a song from the oppressed, who seethe
obligingly sing in tongues about the dream

of lifting up their captor's infants
and happily dashing their skulls against the rocks.

Six Little Hymn-like Jokes to the Night

And now I awaken, for I am both yours and mine.
— Novalis, *Hymns to the Night*

1.

Nighttime is my time
to paint these prison walls
with schools of cloud-bright minnows
atop a wash of cerulean-blue

time to light the black candle
of this panopticon tower, make it blaze
like lady liberty's torch.

2.

Or maybe nighttime
is the best time to blink awake
like a grain of sand
twitching through
    the
    neck
of an hourglass about
                                        to fall

off the oak escritoire
of a late-Victorian beekeeper
whose art is a kind of science

and whose science is the kind of art
that regrets nothing, remembers nothing, hears
nothing other than his hive's singular love
of night.

3.

Nighttime means nothing
the way a saguaro forest means something
during the day, when I least expect it to —

swells of viridescent fire rolling over the earth
toward foothills of black basalt
and bright-edged bodies of water, meaning

the breached limits of finitude, meaning
my overflowing desire for a little more
of everything — prestige, power

the Las Vegas slot machine jingle
which is the sound
of my own name, meaning

the undiluted sweetness
and unambivalent Apollonian spotlight
beaming down upon those

with perfect looks
and perfect vision
except at night.

4.

Like a heartless archer
shooting billionaires up
into target-less space, nighttime is betting
their rockets re-enter a world other
than the one we helped them build

then toss aside, ecstatic
at the chance they might not land so
safely — that all their firebrand, trailblazing glory
ends with night burning brighter
than day.

5.

Back on Earth
late August, at dawn or dusk, a bee

finds itself imprisoned
between the venetian blinds

and the window's cool glass
its fuzzy skull tap-tap

tapping like the hog-bristle tip
of a painter's brush on dry canvas.

The bee's name, by the way
is Chris Hutchinson.

So I say thanks, Chris, thanks
for the big brash colours of your heart

and for the tiny Hindenburg of your career
in the literary arts:

fiat nox.

6.

And soon, it will be nighttime
again, which means time

for untranslatable
shadows

and for the fridge to hum
its nocturn.

And What of the Fleshy Contents of My Skull?

These cumulus clouds
are empty thought balloons
in a comic book about life
in the eternal present no one
has time to read.
        Beneath this rust-
red trestle bridge, the river froths
and foams, pale green like the flesh
of the honeydew melon (*Cucumis melo*)
I tried to eat this morning, but too soon
before its name had fully plumped itself
        into Being's
                beatitude!
Now it's noon, and I'm walking with the sun
perpendicular to the river's rushing
water forever whispering its way
into and out from the mind's ear-
shaped estuaries and bays.
        Just moments before, my mind —
which still isn't working
right — had rippled along the shore
along with summer's late surprise
at all the crumbling eyesores, the extant rows
of redbrick cottages left vacant and half-
shadowed by groves of poplar (*Populus balsamifera*)
whose leaves I want to say are like the fat
curvilinear eyes and cheeks
of Renaissance cherubim!
        All I'm saying is, everywhere
there's empirical evidence
of empyreal design, there's something
to see, something to know, something

to live for? Or maybe
I've just been duped into thinking
this way, ever since the morning Adam
first awoke, feeling denotative, proprietary
and vaguely American — how, before he begot
or bit the fruit, his mouth was already full
of worldly appellations.
        And maybe I'm wondering
if all this naming didn't also colonize
our imaginations, slowing the swift-
flowing waters of *kisiskāciwani-sīpiy*
into the "North Saskatchewan River"
curtailing its current of syllables, soothing
its spumy vowels into something easier
to ignore? *But this is not your river*
        and not your place
to say, the clouds are whispering inside
my head. They're telling me
the epistemic joke that language likes
to tell itself must eventually fall
flat. They're saying this bridge will rust one day
and call it quits, along with the *fleshy*? *pulpy*? *spongy*?
contents of my skull — *kersplash!*
        But not before
the poplar's leaves yellow, almost
bursting into flame, then come fluttering down
like so many clever hands severed
        from their wrists —
yet still trying to write, spinning around
their quill-like stems as if to inscribe the air
with a few last words before
they skim the water's surface
        find purchase there and let the river take them ...

And What of the Dyslexic Skywriter?

He leaves all
his big decisions to chance —
his cowardice seasoned with a salty dash
of fly-by-night recalcitrance.

On days off, he heads to the discount mall
in his blue silk pajamas and signature red scarf.
He likes to jog in place and flap his arms
on the broken escalator until
security comes to ask him
to *please move along.*

Next, depending on the barometric pressure
inside his head, he either cruises to the food court
and fills his pockets with straws, napkins, and ketchup packs
or he glides into Peoples Jewellers and acts
the shy aspiring bridegroom sizing-up
diamond cuts and carats.

About a year ago, he'd been hired to spell
WILL YOU MARRY ME, MARK? above
the city's jagged prospect.
But at 8,000 feet the sun, reflecting off his starboard wing
kept slicing his instrument panel
into prismatic ribbons, and at 12,000 feet
he felt a migraine winding up the spring
of his dyslexia.

And so, on his last day of skywriting
from the hot exhaust of his trusty Cessna Aeronaut
he uncoiled, in bold cursive loops of smoke
WILL YOU MARK ME, MARY?

Was it fate, or did he do this to himself?

After the mall, at home
he likes to flit like a sparrow
between cable news channels while scrolling
on the endless runway of his phone, playing dice
with his mind's attention, flipping coins
with his own intentions, and reneging
every time he loses, which is almost
every time.

These days, he's got days
off for miles and miles ...

Skywriting was a whim anyway —
a wrong-way-up prairie view he fell into
by simply closing his eyes.
At best, it was a vocation, but never
a profession, nothing solid
he could stand on.

And according to his ex-wife, Mary
he would find clarity and purpose
and return to *terra firma* only if
he first found a psychotherapist
covered by his insurance.

Does he have that kind of insurance?
Does he really think escalators can fly?
And who dumped all these bleeding ketchup packs onto
the robin-egg credenza his ex-wife left behind?

Furthermore, the skywriter wonders, whatever
happened with his last client's nuptial plans?
What *was* her name, that would-be bride-to-be?

Was it a coincidence? Was it really "Mary" who forced the issue
and popped the question, or did he fill in the blank
canvas of the sky that day with the cursive loops
of his own future
undoing?

But maybe it was for the best:
His scrambled *WILL YOU MARK ME, MARY?*
suggestive of scars to come, thus triggering
the never-to-be groom to take off, forewarned
and unscathed?

Yes, the skywriter thinks, maybe
he *is* a fly-by-night hero of sorts — albeit
inverted and looking backwards. Maybe in a previous life
he was unmarried, free of Earth's surly grammars
and accountable to no one — a child
born of no parents, a godlike

daredevil poet of the skies!

By now, he knows
how they know him at the mall
by a name that's not his own — a name
he carries with him like his favourite scarf.
By now, he's ready to go:

Tonight, he'll toss the sticky ketchup packs
along with the credenza, but he'll keep
his pilfered straws and napkins, and with tape and scissors
fashion a model of his hero's famous triplane.
(By chance, he'd found the step-by-step instructions
while scrolling on his phone.)

Tomorrow, he'll take the elevator up
to the fourth-floor mezzanine — where he'll either test fly
his paper glider or, depending on the barometric pressure
launch himself over the balustrade
and laughing, flap his arms.

Carrying on, Carrying Over

When I say *happiness,* I mean
stop talking.

When I say *others*, I mean
keep going until you're lost.

When I say *goodnight, kill the lights*, I mean
not sex or death, but convenience is my secret god

and now the cat wants out again.

When I say *sunrise,* I mean
maybe tomorrow.

When I say *moonlight,* I mean
what happened to yesterday's
grotesque burlesque?

Listen, when I say *river*
the *meaning* of a river
is what I mean

which is impossible to articulate
without saying *lightning lays down*
it smooth green bones to sleep.

When I say *dream,* I have to admit
I've never stepped into a river — not even once.

TWO

No butterfly collector
can trap light or detect where
the darkness dwells.

— Joseph Brodsky (trans. George L. Kline)

This is Not a Poem

Effortlessly as this blue
white-streaked marble

drifting between the sun's
shivering gold

and the moon's
fiery silver

slipping like Van Gogh's cypresses
through night's wilding stars

tripping in the channel between desire
and pleasure —

we, our unborn souls like translucent green-winged butterflies, get away
with (almost) everything!

The elderly, childish
and lazy, are just pretending to be old.

Can't they see? They're just pretending
not to see. They're not even trying.

They walk so slowly. Have they forgotten
how to walk, how to run?

Us kids, we can see and walk and run
so easily.

We face the world so keenly
so clearly that the world must

look on us, and sing and celebrate us
exclusively!

The elderly have violated this pact.
They've lost their youth's promissory note —

The world is yours! All the possibilities!
It's their fault. They got old

because they forsook (there's an old word)
something — something they once vowed

never to give up, like how to live
for the body's tasselled embarrassment

of sensory delights, for the soul's
soap bubble rainbow reflection

of itself!

Other than growing
taller and stronger

and stronger and
becoming absolutely

committed to truth
beauty and revolutionary

Democratic Socialism —
what else is there?

Too soon, our green naïveté
cracks like a seed's husk, a resinous ache
oozing, and a wilderness rooting
down into the earth's labyrinth

and what was once light and true
becomes heavy, knotted, angularly
misaligned.

In the time it takes
a butterfly's soul
to transmigrate
our wilderness contracts
to a cultivated career
our hours and days
to a series of teeth-
clenching chores.

More adverb than verb
our mind.

More adjective than noun
our body.

Our life
ancillary, defined

by what makes the world
go 'round.

Each small kiss
just another x on the evening's
schedule of events.

Too soon, our neck stoops
like a banker's lamp —
head dimly totaling
sums and deficits.

Our vision films over —
a grainy, slow-motion movie
of sinking
to the bottom
of a silted lake.

And *hearing* — ?

The Pissing Evil.
Neuropathy.
Kidney failure.
Un-Miltonic
retinopathic blindness.
The green disinfectant-mixed-with-piss-
and-cafeteria-smell of hospitals.

Etcetera.

Me? at forty-nine
but for the grace of god-
knows-what

I'm not there
yet (or maybe I am

depending on when
you're reading this.

Maybe I'm here
only in vestigial
traces, the poem
a reliquary).

No, I'm not there yet, but last month
my father died.

The whir
of his art and politics
has quieted.

The lights and shadows
of his truths, half-truths
and well-meaning lies
have fled.

The tapestry
of his work, family, and love
has come
undone.

The palimpsest depths
of his face, and all the surface traces
the creases, whiskers, scars
the one pale mole cresting his brow
like a small moon —
gone.

His face is gone
but for the few features
mostly around the eyes
he left to me.

In my eyes
in the mirror

I see his eyes
see my face

is crumbling.

What have *I* forsaken?

It's a hard bloody life

I hear him, half-jokingly, say.
Quit your pissing and moaning!

I guess we die because we have to —
this truth we intuit

as an egregious, irrefutable
error.

I guess we die because all forms
must return to the formless void
of their origins —

the nameless father of all
who is all that is, all that's not

the set that contains all sets
that can't but somehow must
contain itself

the invisible, inviolate chapters
the reader invents after
the novel's end

not the centre's roiling vortex
but the stars *outside* the frame
of *Starry Night* —

I guess.

((((·))))

And as I turn my face
toward that other mirror
which is this page
with its facsimiles of grief

I find myself
asking:

Will my absolute
commitment to poetry
flicker?

Will it rage
or whimper?

Will I chase the living moment, hook it
from the sky, then take it home to fix a pin

beneath its lidless compound eye
(at the logocentric point of what this poem's *about*)?

((((·))))

But this is not a poem.
        It's not a eulogy, or a portrait, or a butterfly.

This is just me
        pissing and moaning

over everything poetry
        refuses to signify, me

gnashing my teeth
        at the serifed edge

of eloquence
        where words

half-revealing
        half-concealing

make and break
        their promises.

((((·))))

When I was young
        poetry was a young man's game

of pretending to know the difference
        between *pretext* and *pretense*

between truth and self-
        deceiving artistry

and what, if anything
        happens at the end

of suffering. I admit
        as a kid

I could never face the world
        but I could close my eyes

and trace its absence
        so keenly, so clearly —

this secret I tried to keep
          even from myself.

Now, I'm old enough
to say, this is not a poem
yet. Poems don't exist
until we close the book
and walk (or fly)
away.

THREE

Tears fall from the castles around my heart.

— RiFF RAFF

Aurora Borealis

The child absorbs
his mother's milk
and the blood-
cracked whites
of his father's eyes.

Quiet as the moment
before creation
the child intuits
what comes next —

the frozen river's
tempting innocence
the hare's caramel-coloured coat
turned to reflect all wavelengths
of visible light, a brightening
galactic plane above, and the ice-
cream-lid of the moon
sealed tight.

What the Earth absorbs
the child can't always see —
the dead in their sinking boats
neutrinos, cosmic rays
and even at night, Apollo's
magnetically twisted
personality radiates
fields of love
and hate.

So now the child observes
through his bedroom window
the darkness turn
to a murmuration of candied starlings
feathering into silken vermilions
and translucent jades.

Now he hears his parents fighting
in some other dark, then far away
yet all around, there's the crack
of uncreation, the frozen river split
open by a god-sized fist.

Obscurity

Glory is fleeting, but obscurity is forever.
— Napoleon Bonaparte

There's no coming back or down
from the tippy-top of this cell tower's antenna

there's only a view of storm clouds gathering
greyish-blue like the bruises

from my nurse's clumsy
venipuncture.

And there's no tipping point
at the pointy end of a hypodermic, or bayonet —

just a quick slick ride all the way
through the flesh, then on to fame or shameful

obscurity — or so Napoleon said
but never actually held as true.

At home, in her sanitized condo, loafing
in her furry orca suit, my nurse accepts

that all the world's a hospice. We're all here
to die. Her question is, how to snatch the last

pearl of pleasure from the underwater level
of the Coral Mall's Apple Store without

admitting she's lonely, and lives in Burnaby now.
Napoleon moved from Corsica

when he was nine. At 35, he crowned himself
Emperor and abolished dauphins, loitersacks

and feudal goons. Yet in his dreams he planted
not a single mango tree, and the noun *propagule* remained

as foreign to him as the ice-cream-cone-like corals
at the bottom of the Coral Sea — thus, he kept

the Red Man of the Tuileries close to his chest
like a second heart.

My nurse (whose name, let's imagine
is Josephine) comes up for air.

At night, the lights of Burnaby
are the colour of gentrified piss.

She's on her condo's rooftop, at the edge
of her cell provider's network

which is a festering boil
of panic. Everywhere, the world is suffering

from penetrating cardiac trauma.
The greyish-blue skies are leaking

and even the oceans are slowly
bleeding to death.

She holds her phone aloft
like she's offering the moon, nosing

from the clouds, a lick from an ice cream cone
(let's enforce coherence, let's go all the way

and say it's mango-flavored, just like her own
sweetly detached and erotically propagating

self). But as she shuffles closer
to the tower, I see her bare feet sticking out

from her furry orca tail as if
the whale she wants to be

is giving birth to something all
too human. Me?

No, I didn't make it.
I'm at the tippy-top of a crematorium stack

like a smoky pearl of wasted ejaculate.
There's no coming down or back.

At the end, the Little Corporal said:
La France, l'armée, tête d'armée, Joséphine.

I say, glory's overrated.

Moving in Alone

There are some defeats more triumphant than victories.
— Michel de Montaigne

Is there a pill I could take
that would make me less afraid
of you, less in love, less enraged?

Your best poetry now sounds
like a purple, semi-literate jumble
of idiolects and popular trash

clothed in glittery Velcro
sticking together and ripping
apart and rolling all over the floor

of some afterhours comedown party
back in 1994. I'm not complaining
about wasted time, or words

winking in space, graceful
and painless as the opalescent foam
decanting from the mouth

of a soap bubble blower a lifetime
ago. I'm just saying
the shiny pellets

the prestige economy
dispenses to the already
peacockishly self-

gratified are always just
out of reach. So I am complaining, a bit.
Why? Because I spent my whole life

hammering sheets of darkness into difficult
shapes, by which I mean making up lies disguised
as verities, and avoiding the world's bright

sticky webs. I wasted my prime
concocting semantic contraptions worthy
of Rube Goldberg's repressed

inner life, and you don't seem
to care! How many rooms did I build
how many labyrinths of doubt

each enclosing at least one
tortuously wrought intellectual-slash-
emotional grotesquerie — the image

of a black moonbeam, let's say
prying open the mind's sarcophagus! —
which only two or three souls

would ever chance to read, let alone
live by, or die for, or adopt
on their syllabus. But maybe I needed it

this way, to stay hidden, meaning
unassailable, beyond reproach.
Luckily, there were pills for everyone

to swallow, pills for any and all
occasions, some bitter, some bitterly
sweet, i.e. erotic —

one for every year I still want
to curse, one for every greased braincell
that writhed and wept in verse —

pills, by which I mean dust mote
shadows, black insects of punctuation, and stars
the size of pores inked into my skin.

I mean pixels, sunspots, floaters, souls of dead bumblebees
and the future's florescent eye glaring like the nipple
of a crumpled piece of cellophane.

And where were you at the end
of last century? Were you living on one mustard seed
a day, talking to yourself

in the voices of imaginary saints
and secretly drinking, ounce by ounce
whole rivers and oceans of rage?

Were you spending all your strength
and spilling all your sweetness, your body
like a cracked alabaster flask?

Were you sacrificing sense
for the half-heard roar
of your own blood?

Let's say we both agreed
we needed the other
gone in order to survive.

Let's say to not kill ourselves
we spited, disdained
and wrote.

And maybe I was happier
back when I was miserable
because lonelier.

Maybe it was simpler for me
to be so difficult. Harder for you
to make it look so easy.

We Thieves

Like this handsome magpie, we've returned
from places no one can prove
we've ever been.

Like the hulls of medieval galleons full
of nothing but anchors and mooring chains
we creak and groan.

We whisper *verily*
and your freckles rearrange.

We mouth the shapes
and sounds of sawdust blooms
hot soldering irons, and midnight frosts.

We arise, break
the mountain's back
flow in twisted ropes of molten rock
then stiffen, cooling into grooves
of past eruptions.

We pluck white whiskers
from the tails of comets
squeeze stars
like zits.

We fill the space
between wolf and moon, no
not with howls, but with ifs
and buts and whys and who
knows whats.

We fly our colours
under the radar, propeller blades
appearing then disappearing then blurring
into a semi-transparent
porthole in the sky.

Along with the ocean
we feel the rain, plinking
with the same finger
over and over and over
again, may be the answer
to the questions: who
is Philip Glass, and what
was he thinking?

Don't worry, the love we make
is quiet as the oiled hinge
of a dragonfly's wing
quiet as the fluorescent textures
of atoms you miss
when we blink.

We say *Hwæt!*
and your follicles concentrate.

We live where you won't touch
pray for that which you can never be
or do unless you're willing

like a good little colonialist

to give this magpie a top hat
and a fat gold pocket watch to match
his brand-new stolen tuxedo.

Fire, Honey, and Ice

Some say the world will end in fire,
Some say in ice.
— Robert Frost

Climbing through
frozen mists, the sun, at its zenith
is the colour of a brimstone moth, itself
the colour of honey made from bees sated
on clover. Because nothing goes on
unaffected, all my mentors are dead
or gone to beekeeping. In their apiaries
they soothe their hives with the white incense
of burning cedar chips. They puff their bellows
and genuflect beneath all the ways the sun
with its zillion tongues of honey
with its zillion fiery wings
hates hyperbole. No word ever says
exactly what it means, which is why
my mentors prefer the poetry
of honeybees. They know *hive*
can also mean *rash*, which has nothing to do
with the collective mind, unless we're talking
irrational urges — not inside
the tangible world (which includes
the sweetly aromatic smoke of the dead)
but within these hot flickers of icy hate
that can sting, or give life
like the word *love* that lives
in *clover*.

A Family Outing

Everyone loves Mother-of-pearl
but ignores Pearl's stepfather.
He's the one standing in the middle of the crowded gallery

holding an empty cup as if it's full of saltwater about to
spill. Is it himself or the joke
of himself he's clinging to

and hiding behind, and wanting no one
to disturb? (No one asks this question
but me, and I'm not here.)

She's the one featured and framed
in the painting before him: Mother-of-pearl
wearing her nacreous headdress

which artfully borders and elongates and streams
down her face, lifting her status above the medieval
pilgrims and fisherfolk.

Meanwhile, the daughter feels the evening
taking on the protracted sting and boredom
of a family outing. Everyone here's annoying

and wants something from her, their glances pressing in
and the air hissing like a wave pulling back from shore, dragging
unseen microplastics mixed with grains of feldspar and quartz.

So she retreats to the cramped security
of a bathroom stall and sheds
expensive tears.

Her mother, when she was still alive
liked to call her father
"a broken shell of a man."

But Pearl remembers his salt-crusted beard
and his eyes — sunken, but fiery with rum
like tidal pools reflecting the midday sun.

Meanwhile, the stepfather has left
the building, and is travelling inland
at great rate of speed.

(I'm still not here, but I have questions
about the mother's passing, right after I captured her image
in iridescent oils, over five hundred years ago.)

Event Horizon

You're always standing here
like how a room stands
inside itself. You're floating in air

like the angel of air
inside of aerogel.
You're pretending to be

meek-eyed, easy-going, detached
from history. But your thoughts and prayers
will soon require

thoughts and prayers
if you ever hope to win me
with your affections, or should I say

wound me with your *affectations*
of love. Like blue-eyed Jesus on the cross
you've aligned your true identity

with the living silence.
You say there's nothing here to hear
or see, just a prairie night sky's

parable of punctuation — each spangled point
of light not a bullet hole, but a zygote's full stop.
Then, the embryonic comma unfurling

its tail — within its hesitation, a hint
of movement, a twitch prefiguring time, and the expanding syntax
of a sentence inside a galaxy of sentences

all revolving around some sacred fulcrum
too far away to be observed, too vast
to be ignored.

All the while, your grammar
is gendered, unpopular, needy.
Like gravity, it puts demands on everyone.

Even light bends accordingly and the line's resolve breaks
under its own encumbrance like a branch overladen with fruit
and erotic connotations. Or should I say *conventions* —

those unholy relics that govern the passions
that govern us. So yes, maybe you exist
(by which I mean Jesus lives in Tulsa

Oklahoma at the corner of Quincy Ave.
and Route 66) and maybe it's me who's make-believe —
a literally fictitious citizen of the world

in exile, yet still subject
to your geography, cosmology, religion, and dead
semantic weight.

If so, there's no escape.
Each poem I write imprisons me here
and sets you free.

Breakfast at the Armory Hotel in Bozeman, Montana

Somewhere in the future
from inside the antique armoire
inside the Armory Hotel, the future
is looking back at me.

But not before I peer in
at the sequences of switchbacks
and figure eights, the puzzling
tunnels and galleries
of the worm-inscribed
mahogany.

It looks like someone tried
to write a sonnet
on a roller coaster
with one finger.

Deciphered and sonified
it is the underground lighthouse
sound of ringing in my ears.

As a figure of speech
that got lost along the way
to the doomsday parade
it is the horizon's feathery fringe that blinks
when the sky closes its big blue eyes
to sleep.

As real as the fact of my own birth
as certain as the place / time coordinates
of my final breath

and better

than any superlative exaltation
it is like frying a quail's egg
but burning the butter

like the recurring dream they have up here
in Montana, of lassoing bulls with ropes
woven from mulberry silk.

Elongated, Waterworn Sonnet

for M.L. Martin

They came from the west, from the skies
above Millcreek Ravine — clouds, darkening
each leaf, removing each grass blade's
bent silhouette. I wasn't there. But the river was
and it made little coyote-like leaps over its favourite boulder
shaped like a heart. Then it purled and pooled
and in the sandy shallows, fell asleep. It dreamt
of me dreaming of you reading this page
incredulously. You'd hoped to see dragonflies reeling
and unreeling like drunken royalty above waters
that knew all there was to know of their own distances
and depths. Instead, you found me lost
in the word *pearlescent* as a way to involve
not the dragonfly's wings, but the sound of the river forever
clearing these small smooth stones from its throat.

FOUR

We live on the circumference of a hollow circle. We draw the circumference, like spiders, out of ourselves: it is all criticism of criticism.

— Laura Riding Jackson

What I Know Isn't What I Want to Know

When, at the designated viewing spot
we look off into the view
how many of us are seeing the view?

My life's so far behind it thinks
it's outstripping the sun. Each place replaced
by the image of a place.

My seesaw tilts east, then falls
back under the weight of the present moment's collapsing
infinities.

Next, out west, the Pacific breathes and I think
I hear the colours of its tongue and throat, taste the future
with its lips as they sip the rocky shore.

Each image transfixed
inside the idea of an image. And how many of us
are just pretending?

Meanwhile, Myrmidons

Clouds float by
like the distracted thoughts
of underpaid lab technicians.

Their hypothesis is
thoroughbred enlightenments
breed rough lichens.

Meanwhile, the flushed faces of myrmidons
appear in the rear view mirror, grotesque
like half-formed similes —

We mean what we say
when we say we say
what we mean

they say
to themselves
without really meaning to

before they can listen.

According to the Art of Hunger

> *Art means nothing if it simply decorates the dinner table of the power which holds it hostage.*
> — Adrienne Rich

Your resubmitted treatise on class warfare
has supplanted my feelings
which once tried to spell the word
H-U-N-G-E-R in blood-tipped toothpicks
on the paper plate of the moon.

An evening breeze spins around your oyster mushroom hairstyle.
If they were real, your cheeks might boast a puce filigree of veins.

From this place, Jupiter appears
multiplied in the dragonfly eyes of finance towers
before it rolls across your naked forearm and snags
on a faded razor-wire tattoo.

It's still summer.
Another plinth gets vandalized
by billowing sail-shaped shadows, but then
it's too late. Liberty Island turns red.

How I Ended Up on the Shores of Labrador

for Christopher Brean Murray

All the way over the Rockies, then down
into the smashed-flat prairies, I pursued
the Great Horned Owl of a dream.
My '72 Volvo spewed behind me swarms
of honey-coloured dust beneath a vast cloud
of unknowingness. Pulling into a Motel 6
on the outskirts of Red Deer, I must have appeared
to the other sojourning maniacs to have
nothing on, at least from the waist up.
Appearances are sometimes true. My point is
from the waist down, I could have been
a tree, with all my shameful needs
tensile strengths, and twisted footings
concealed. And, in a violent kind of way
I was. As always, the dream was its own reality
so the question of waking or sleeping
was like reading the blur of intersecting lines
on a map left out in the rain.
It was only when I found myself
alone in my room, waltzing around and singing
off-key: *Am I or am I not the Steve Buscemi*
of Canadian poetry? that I realized I was
turning and turning, with predatory intent
in narrowing circles above my own
smashed-in head. I decided then
to uproot my life, to sever all ties.
I'd check out early and drive, goddammit
all the way east in one straight burn, hungover
and cursing myself for having failed to ask
the beautiful receptionist to help me

locate my courage on my wet, blurry map.
To this day, I can still see their owlish eyes
like unfathomable pools reflecting the light
with terrible clarity — a light whose source
I'd never know. Was it destiny? At Crossfield
I took a wrong turn in the rain, then my Volvo
broke down five miles from Medicine Hat
where I was soon to discover my next true identity.

Don't Follow Me

Certius esset et verum si semper esset mentiendi regula
— Cicero

Walking this labyrinth and speaking in riddles, I say
painting is to vision what memories are to ribbons
of scent. Moreover, photography is to light what fishing line is
to fast-running waters (or so said Ansel Adams to Richard Brautigan
back when they were never friends). And at the centre of sleep
there's dreaming, like dancers inside of music.

And because you are whispering to yourself, it's dusk again.
The horizon, if you must look, is an electrified greenish-gold wire.
The cottonwoods are lousy with magpies, raucous in their stolen tuxedos.
Their cries, like the creak of old machinery, but less devotional
their cries, like rusted closeline pulleys, screeching
under the mundane beauty of the everyday life

you left out to dry — Are you with me?
This labyrinth offers various pathways and choices.
For instance, either poetry is to language
what philosophy is to thought
or the wording of this analogy will lead you
to ruinous conclusions.

Triumvirate

for Marc di Saverio

Me, myself, and thy
subjunctive mood disorder would resist
the élan of imperial magnificence

but after the apotropaic archways collapse, to be reclaimed
as rubbleworks of volcanic stone at the foot of Roman Gaul

and after the Language Police build their crooked laws
inside someone's beautifully curved mouth, mine
or yours, whoever's is more eloquent

than factual (as if you could betray me
by betraying yourself, kicking at grammars

beneath this ruined city), then the locust-shapes
of my ideographic mistakes would appear fixed
their iridescent wings making stately geometric designs

and the outthrust antennae resembling a net
burst open with conquests, triumphs, spoils

expanding to an immeasurable thinness, all
conjunctions forgone in the scattering debris.
"Nothing's good unless it lasts forever," you used to say.

Thus *thus* — as if I'd never heard the Emperor's echoing words.
As if you were only stammering from the darkening outskirts.

Nietzsche …

Nietzsche Nietzsche Nietzsche Nietzsche Nietzsche …
Why can't the man ever
shut up?

Why must he
over and over, keep
coming back?

Imagine the colour
of the colour black before
he was born.

Untitled in a World Called Money, Beauty, Fame

Poets die adolescents.
— Robert Lowell

The artist is extremely lucky who is presented with the worst possible ordeal which will not actually kill him. At that point, he's in business.
— John Berryman

On Day One, Larry-the-Lizard quits smoking and eating saturated crap.
Day Two: he buys a hard pack of Dunhill King Size
on his way to Fatty Patty's Burger Palace. Why?
Because the purplish overcast sky has cracked open
along the horizon like a cauldron lid beneath which roils
an elvish, golden-green, late July twilight.
He's no climatologist — *but!*
Maybe he's what they call neurodivergent?
Maybe he'll shave his eyebrows in order to become less
human, more alien to himself, and hence more professionally
objective during faculty meetings?
On Day Three, Larry-the-Liz is tip-toeing in his Jordans
up the hill's cranium when he spots the man himself —
that Boston Brahmin dressed in a rumpled camelhair overcoat.
Yes, it's Robert Lowell, paused along the promenade
and leaning out over the guardrail toward the river valley
where divisions of darkness are slowly disassembling
and reassembling and coming in and out of wispy existence
like all of his secret wishes in some afterhours subterranean dive.
Thrusting up and away from Daddy Lowell's wilting shoulders
a pair of blue-black, blade-shaped wings shimmer
and flash in the thickening, ageless, adjectival air.
On Day Four, conjured by the buzz of an awakening
sodium lamp, Mr. Skunk-Hour's shadow pools
at his heels. At first, taking the form of a sleeping lion

the shadow quickly morphs into a global financial crisis
then bursts into flame. Our reptilian protagonist
shudders. He's no eschatologist — *but!*
Day Five, and Larry-Larry-Quite-Contrary, while sipping cherry-
flavored mescaline, decides to smoke half a chewed-up Bolivian
cigar. But when he does, when he sets the charred nub alight
Bolivia erupts. *And yet!* — the miraculous fact that Larry exists
or that anyone or anything exists, is, in and of itself, still, somehow
not enough. Dear reader, here's the ironical part:
familiarity with himself, via the chronic introspection
which his vocation both feeds and aggravates
has made our chameleon hero virtually invisible
to himself, and now, staring into his vintage empire
mirror, he sees only what's most tragically obvious, namely
the sheer sum total of all he is not. Which is a lot.
For example, he isn't rich, beautiful, or famous — not yet, not *yet!*
Day Six: after reviewing and mulling over his progress
then chowing down on a whole package of Crinkle Cut Oven Fries
plain-ol'-Larry admits that tomorrow, it's back to Day One.
Meanwhile, the sky's lid is pressing down again with the weight
of a sixth mass extinction. It's about to steal him away
seal him in for good, along with his very next decision
or his inability to make a decision. More than ever, Larry feels
an endless series of lead-sinkers dragging him under, all the years
he can't, or won't, endure. But, dear onlooker, dear fetishist
of the woefully obscure, here's the unwritten (until now) truth:
If words fell from trees then money would be useless
and beauty and fame would become a kind of homelessness
made entirely of starlings whipping and weaving above all
the empty parking lots of Eastern Massachusetts.
Meanwhile, that neurasthenic ghost, levitating on the ballpoint tips
of his knife-edged wings, pivots and transforms
into a shadow of his friend, the poet, John Berryman.
The Dream Songs' dreamer's dark eyebrows leap into space as he steps
over the guardrail — urged by a force older than gravity —
and waves.

Creation

The word
divides, then
the world

encroaches
and history's sparkling tide
of cruelty.

Ra becomes Zeus, then Ovid
approaches and appropriates
the entire Greek universe
etcetera.

Fast forward.

At this rate, the human population
will soon surpass the mass
of the entire known universe.

Wherever I am
it's always darker, brighter
wherever I'm not.

Stop.

The Dying Art of Healthcare

A single filament filibusters through the night
arguing that sumptuary laws, when closing the door

should admit no warm watery light. Inside
the freezer's nocturne, you think you hear an oboe's

aubade, even as you watch the words "oboe"
and "aubade" lifting from the page of your recent attempts

to revise "The Dying Art of Healthcare."
Promises, promises. If only these soft platelets

would harden and close your public profile
at this newly privatized heart transplant clinic

then you might reset the clock of sanguinity
ticking beneath the skin of post-everything-ism

and settle back into your vintage ball turret
gunner's chair like a moral cynosure for future

generations. If only. If only there were more to art
than suturing each red impulse with dopamine loops

more to each day than *getting and spending* —
then spending each evening sealed up inside

the cold seed of your body — like dying alone
in perfect physical condition.

Against Translation

Never move to a village where the women speak Old Gaelic
in their sleep. Instead, drift along inside this animal skin boat

framed in wickerwork and say the weeping willows are the river's
veiled brides. Or say they're not and bow to every green impulse

to plunge into the lyric's declensions, which is to say, learn to read
the image behind the antique symbol. Sure, the river is pure

unbraided muscle, though only when thought of from afar
or from a fear of the virtuosic turns your dream invents

against your will but for your betterment by all these mazy ways
of suffering. Such fear is justified and, like a marriage

can't easily be undone. So, as the village floods with breath
soft as bed sheets warmed from sleep, be sure to choose

more modern idioms. But speak them only
to yourself, unconjugated

inside your coracle.

Being-There

You'd think vanilla swimwear would be
the envy of chocolate statuary.

You'd think psychedelic lichens would mean more
interest in four-player chess as a metaphor

for the imminent demise
of Meta.

You'd think someone would've said something
else about the *lone and level sands*

stretching out beyond the shadows
of our transient endeavours.

But, as you — who
on a cold bench facing the river valley

feeds an albino squirrel
crumbs of stale coffee cake —

as you might say — you
meaty man of valour

you beetle-in-a-box owner
you lover of the word "moreover" —

as you might say to no one
but this ghostly squirrel with eyes

the colour of watery drops
of blood —

Look on my works, ye mighty
and disambiguate!

Because, according to you
the truth is never not

everywhere.

Dear Futurists, I'm a Futurist Too, in Spirit

Like me, you want everything to be
given to you, including those argon-blue particles

that haunt the other side, the ghostly side of this trans-
parent skin between worlds.

Welcome to the back of the mind's
smartphone, wherein lithium wars, pandemics, and unexpected

roaming fees await. If you complain
I'll say, take a weeping pill and cry

yourself to sleep. I'll say, I was crushing Pong
zonked on Fruit Loops when you were still

a bunch of scattered atoms
without a cosmos. Check this out:

It was a dark and stormy Karaoke Nite
the night my crystal cruise ship of a soul slipped

past resemblance like ...
Like you, I can't hang on to thoughts.

I shiver, lost without a style with which to signify
nothing, but adverbially *mean* it.

Cancel that. Ctrl Alt Delete. Unsend.
Unfriend. What I meant to say is

I'd like to play the internet like a centipede
plays the flute, which is the earth

that trills beneath its feet. Wouldn't you?
No, I'm not following you either because

I'm a forty-nine year-old man
and according to the algorithm, you still live

with your girlfriend's boyfriend's
grandmother. I know we're both sorry

not sorry. I also know that whoever
touches this poem — mine or yours —

touches a touchscreen.
No one's alone.

The Spell of the Yukon (2001)

I wanted the gold, and I sought it;
I scrabbled and mucked like a slave.
Was it famine or scurvy — I fought it;
I hurled my youth into a grave.
— Robert Service, "The Spell of the Yukon"

Where was New York when I found myself living
in a nylon tent outside Dawson City, beside the Yukon River
beneath a sky twisted with birch limbs, and barely surviving
on booze, bad luck, and the summer sun's everlasting light?
Amongst the crows and the ravens — whom I took pains to describe
as "obstreperous" and "grandiloquent," respectively, noting
how they juddered, strutted, and disdained one another
staking their ritual turf — in the midst of such pseudo-religious
skirmishes, I wondered: where was that infallible
fact? The one I might find locally distilled, the colour
of its feverish perfume carved in stone — which is to say
pure gold? At once too shy and too cunning to think a mere smile
and a wink might win me a dance with Diamond Tooth Gertie
(who just so happened to be the Sherriff's daughter and queen
of the philological underground), I slithered, slowly
and with a blurred sense of purpose, into and out from my tent
of hebetude. How I possessed and caressed my hebetude!
I owned it like the Oxford Dictionary owns the collected works
of every English poet. (Even these lines were written there
first, pre-incarnate, in another form.) Thus, to flip randomly
through pages was to bear witness to an unfolding
of accidents dressed up as art. (Have I said all this
before?) I even began reading into the miniscule holes
in the stitching of my tent: adding up each mosquito bite
of light, halving the sum to account for my whiskey-
split vision, dividing by one, thinking, God

was I really this far north, this alone? — then blacking-
out. The next day, I looked up "hebetude" in my pocket
Oxford, only to discover I was too slothful to turn
the requisite number of pages, let alone comprehend.
Who knows why, but that's when I decided
I didn't love words, or gold, or Gertie's diamond-toothed grin.
No, I loved New York, and longed for all its geniuses
and bedlamites fighting for relevancy and scudding across
famous bridges without me — even though, at this stage
in my peripatetic career, I'd never laid eyes on that city
except for the ten thousand times it had appeared on TV.
Hence, my sense of direction was nothing less than an apathetic
landscape boasting one moose-shaped scarp amidst an otherwise
perfectly flat horizon, which was the ever-widening space
of summer's north. You could say I was an impermanent
resident with a near perfect excuse, a hungover prospector
(a hundred years too early, or too late), a man of mystery
without a clue. So, when the sun fell frozen into the river
obviously it was time to go. But first, I dreamt
of Manhattan enveloped in fiery gold, and of ashes black
as a murderous murder of crows flensing and feasting
on a raven's carcass (thus dawned the catastrophe
of my self-awareness). And at the base of a serpentine-limbed
birch tree I awoke with all the eloquence of a stone.

Loneliness is a Condition Institutionally Created and Instated to Control and Subdue the Populace

At the pinnacle of success
work is pure service
without the need to question

or explain the nature of the thing
we find ourselves
most driven to pursue.

In the meantime, the rest of us
follow our bliss
into hell.

The faces of our mother
implicit inside
the faces of our father

whose sanitized hands wield
bright metallic financial
instruments.

At the pinnacle of distress
we understand this analogy
speaks only for itself.

Still, accounts amble.
The ground snaps.
The breach is ruinous.

And when our schemes
dissolve, along with all traces
of their computations

when the signal's lost
when we know ourselves again
as strangers —

The Lonesome Detective

for Jeremy Spohr (1971 - 2010)
searching for Weldon Kees (1914 - 1955?)

Searching for a man who vanished
chasing the one who was loathe to confess

the flaw in his vision, which should have been
his life's work to inspect, along with the theme

that we merely subsist, surrendering
joy in an attempt to avoid suffering —

this friendless detective, fuelled by
Pabst Blue Ribbon and Chet Baker's "Time after Time"

re-reading "Aspects of Robinson"
idolizing "afraid, drunk, sobbing Robinson"

and questioning whether the guise wrote the man
or the man wrote to say, *This is truly who I am*

as night closes over him, his identity
drawn like breath into this other body

his eyes riddled inside the shadowy lines
of a portrait, water stained, black and white —

and soon his suspicions merge
with a confluence of clues so fluid and blurred

that he becomes the one leaving, even asleep
as he falls through a circuitous deep

thrumming with the hollowed-out notes
of an early spring rain, like the pulse behind his throat

in 1955, when a yellow balloon, bobbling
along a cigarette-strewn sidewalk

startles a pair of copulating pigeons, the soft
explosion jolting him, sending him briefly aloft —

until he sees the wind-drubbed balloon
has only scattered the birds into an upside-down view

of his own plummeting ... So much for the life
of the mind, or this other life, the one he blindly

reaches out for. Time's split. He's drunk himself
straight. All the rumours have been dispelled

along with the music, the rain, the echoing street
and the dream within a dream he almost believed

he could live in. But the poet will never come back.
If there was ever a clue, it was in the zodiac

of tire marks and footprints that enshrined
the car deserted beside the sphinxlike bridge — a sign

that what remains is only Robinson.

This Poem Is Uncalled for as the Sun Coming Up or Going Down (2011)

Yet another Sunday sinks
into this hillside mist, then rises

to its own occasion like a long yawn
at noon — and slowly I awake

to trouble, big trouble
trouble with the law, the law

of *Come What May*, of *What's About to Happen*
and so I shut myself within

irrational categories: *Neurotic*
Indecision, Obsessive Packing

and Unpacking, Defining
and Redefining my Point of View:

Here I am, a water-skier
being hauled in circles by some inexhaustible engine

across the onyx-smooth surfaces
of my own disenchantment.

Here I am, a professional indweller
all these thoughts like wounded moths

battering the walls of my internet-
carved skull. Never mind.

In the mirror, opposite the bookshelf
The Poetical Works of John Keats decomposes

to blonde motes of dust and I think I hear
the wet slapping footfalls

of his hidebound critics. I think I'd like to torture
a confession from my oldest poems, self-

conscious lines trembling like votive candles
inside the bombed-out cathedral

of my youth. But no
I will not be comforted or move back

to the last place my spirit
was forced to leave, which —

as my friend and I both agreed
before he began to die

and before I left him there
to get on with it —

which was like a secret outpost
at the edge of some Arizona town

called *Freedom,* called *Surprise,* called *Anything Goes.*
Never mind. Next Sunday

maybe I'll awake to see
the first white lilies

unbuttoning this lonely hillside
and I'll find my way through this valley

to the place I've long longed to live
in poverty, unafraid.

Idyll

> *There are no unsacred places;*
> *there are only sacred places*
> *and desecrated places.*
> — Wendell Berry

Forget white elephants —
instead, let's picture
hills like fluffy clouds
or hills like soft-serve ice-cream
in another, less tragic story
about an arch bridge
where the arches redefine
negative space as blue
cartoon feet. Let's invent
a kinder story
about a fissure in the sky
where a daytime star peeks through
and freezes, a petrified spot
in time. Yes, wherever
this woodland path skirts
the ocean's breezy hip
or a stillness tilts the air
like a compass arrow
on its infinitesimal
pin, that's where
we'll awaken
not so much lost
in an Exxon Mobil
logo's curvatures
or a network of polymer-inspired
pine air fresheners
made to look like mercurial

candy-coloured fish —
but found
in the foreground
which is just distance
from another perspective.
And yes, across a meadow
disguised as the candleflame eyes
of caged lions, through a clearing
in the trees, where August's supple light pauses
like a trapeze artist just before
her final feat, elsewhere, all around
and nowhere, that's where we'll see
these white hills have become —
what? An elephant's ears?
Empty thought balloons?
The sky's pleated pocket square?
Or perhaps they are the happy flags
of our own surrender
to the happy, gentle breeze.

Listen, Believe, Obey

Soon, these lines will subsume
their own measure, just as you must refute

all rumours of their misattribution — lines you'll rewrite
as your body renews its natural energies, styles, and charms

waking up in the morning
falling asleep in my arms.

NOTES

p. 12
"I want to believe I want / all sentient beings / to be free from suffering / and the causes of suffering" presents a cynical revision of the Bodhisattva vow found in Mahayana Buddhism.

p. 15
"DKE" refers to Delta Kappa Epsilon (ΔKE), one of the oldest fraternities in the United States, founded in 1844 at Yale College.

p. 21
The intersection of Main and Hastings at the heart of Vancouver's Downtown Eastside is sometimes called "Pain and Wastings," for obvious reasons.

p. 22
The italicized lines paraphrase Psalm 137:9.

p. 26
The end of "Five Little Hymn-like Jokes ..." borrows from Don McKay's poem "Fridge Nocturn."

p. 40
"The Pissing Evil" is a historical term for diabetes.

p. 43
"... this truth we intuit // as an egregious, irrefutable / error": In *The Gay Science* Friedrich Nietzsche asks, "What then, in the last resort, are the truths of mankind?" and answers: "They are the irrefutable errors [*unwiderlegbaren Irrtüme*] of mankind."

"the nameless father of all / who is all that is, all that's not" rephrases lines from the *Corpus Hermeticum* (V.2. Trans. Copenhaver), a collection of mystical texts allegedly authored by Hermes Trismegistus in late antiquity.

"... the set that contains all sets / that can't but somehow / must contain itself" is a (per)version of Russell's Paradox — named after philosopher and mathematician Bertrand Russell — which emerges from a branch of mathematical logic known as set theory. The paradox occurs with the set that attempts to include all sets but cannot include itself without contradiction.

p. 45
"... where words, // half-revealing / half-concealing // make and break / their promises" steals from Alfred Lord Tennyson's loftier line in *In Memoriam A. H. H*: "For words, like Nature, half reveal // And half conceal the Soul within."

p. 52
"The Red Man of the Tuileries" was a ghost said to haunt the Tuileries Palace in Paris, advising Napoleon on military strategy, but also believed to be an omen of his downfall, as well as that of other rulers before and after him.

p. 54
Moving in Alone is the title of a book by Canadian poet John Newlove (Oolichan Books, 1977).

p. 56
"Were you spending all your strength / and spilling all your sweetness ..." echoes Andrew Marvell's "To His Coy Mistress": "Let us roll all our strength and all / Our sweetness up into one ball."

p. 59
Hwæt! is the first word in *Beowulf*, often translated as "Listen!" or "What!" to grab attention at the beginning of the epic.

p. 79
"Mr. Skunk-Hour" refers to Robert Lowell and his widely anthologized poem "Skunk Hour."

p. 80
"*The Dream Songs'* dreamer" refers to John Berryman and his most celebrated book *The Dream Songs*.

p. 82
The italicized phrase "getting and spending" comes from the famous Wordsworth poem "The World Is Too Much With Us."

p. 84, 85
The phrases "lone and level sands" and "Look on my works, ye mighty!" come from "Ozymandias" by Percy Bysshe Shelley.

p. 87
"No one's alone" steals from Anne Sexton's poem "The Truth the Dead Know."

p. 92
Weldon Kees was an American poet, painter, literary critic, novelist, playwright, jazz pianist, short story writer, and filmmaker. His sudden disappearance in 1955 led to speculation that he may have committed suicide by jumping from the Golden Gate Bridge. "Robinson" was his invented literary persona.

# ACKNOWLEDGEMENTS

For your companionship, wisdom, and support over the years, my heartfelt thanks go to: Chris Banks, Shane Book, Donato Mancini, Maureen Medved, Teresa McWhirter, Christopher Brean Murray, Billeh Nickerson, Steve Noyes, Catherine Owen, Paul Pearson, Matt Rader, and Mark Smith. A special shout-out to Joseph Siddiqi for serendipitously conjuring yet another amazing cover image. As always, my deepest gratitude to M.L. Martin, my companion through all the changes, and my unofficial protector and editor. A huge thanks to my official editor, Jim Johnstone — this book was a collaboration in all the best ways.

And thank you to the editors of the following publications, in which several of the poems in this book appeared, often in earlier forms and under different titles:

The Ampersand Review: "Moving in Alone"
FreeFall Magazine: "Against Translation"
Hobart (US): "Untitled in a World Called Money, Love, and Fame"
Home & Garden (US): Artist Exhibition Catalogue, New York (Curated by Brian Scott Campbell): "What I Know Isn't What I Want to Know," "Idyll"

Literary Review of Canada: "Lost Signal"
Malahat Review: "The Lonesome Detective"
On the Seawall (US): "What I Want Isn't Always What I Want to Want," "And What of the Fleshy Contents of My Skull?"
The Pi Review: "Meanwhile Myrmidons," "According to the Art of Power"
*The Puritan Literary Magazine (*now *The Ex-Puritan)*: "Spell of the Yukon"
The Shore Poetry (US): "Breakfast at the Armory Hotel in Bozeman, Montana"
Several poems from the final section of this book also appeared in the limited-edition chapbook *Meanwhile Myrmidons* and in *The Anstruther Reader* anthology, published by Anstruther Press and Anstruther Books, respectively.

Chris Hutchinson is the author of four previous poetry books, as well as the autofictive verse-novel *Jonas in Frames*. He has lived all over North America, from Dawson City, Yukon, to Brooklyn, New York, working as a line cook and, more recently, teaching creative writing to undergraduates. He is now a permanent faculty member of the English Department at MacEwan University, located on Treaty 6 Territory.